D0841271

Roads to Reasoning

Developing Thinking Skills Through Problem Solving

Suzanne Levin Weinberg

Stephen Krulik

Jesse A. Rudnick

 **Wright Group**
McGraw-Hill

Acknowledgments

Project Editors
Harriet Slonim, Susan McMahon

Writers
Suzanne Levin Weinberg, Stephen Krulik, Jesse A. Rudnick

Design Director
Karen Stack

Cover Design and Illustration
Aki Nurosi

Design
Gerta Sorensen

Illustration
Susan Aiello Studio

Composition
Sorensen London, Inc.

ISBN 0-7622-1347-7
Customer Service 800-624-0822
www.creativepublications.com

5 6 7 8 VHG 07 06 05 04

Contents

Introduction

Rationale

MOST MATHEMATICS EDUCATORS AGREE that the development of reasoning power is a primary objective of elementary mathematics. In fact, problem solving, which is the basis for developing reasoning power, has been at the forefront of the mathematics curriculum for many years. The National Council of Teachers of Mathematics' *Principles and Standards,* released in 2000, continues to emphasize both of these areas. Within the thinking and reasoning domain, the area that requires the greatest attention is the development of higher order thinking skills, specifically critical and creative thinking.

Critical thinking is the ability to analyze a situation and draw appropriate and correct conclusions from the given data.
It also includes determining whether data are inconsistent or if data may be missing or extraneous.

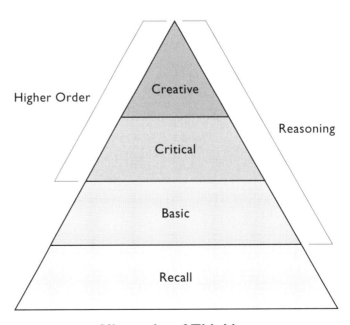

Hierarchy of Thinking

© Wright Group/McGraw-Hill 0-7622-1347-7

Creative thinking is the ability to originate a solution to a problem situation. In addition, it is the ability to generate, synthesize, and apply original ideas to produce a complex product.

Reasoning is the ultimate goal of the books in this series. Problem solving is the road that will lead to an increased ability to reason. The problems in this book are vehicles that carry the students along the road, and the teacher is the driver who guides the students.

Most mathematics textbook series include some degree of problem solving. This series provides additional practice using a variety of approaches that will further develop reasoning power. As children experience a variety of strategies for solving problems, they will become more flexible in their thinking and reasoning.

There is a strong connection between the problems in this series and the language arts—reading, writing, listening, and speaking. Careful reading of a word problem is often as important as mathematical skills for successfully solving the problem. It is critical that children

1) read the problem carefully,

2) find out what they are being asked to do,

3) solve the problem, and

4) determine whether or not the answer makes sense.

What's in This Book?

This book contains six sections, each of which focuses on a specific aspect of the problem-solving process and is designed to strengthen a particular reasoning skill.

Section 1: What Number Makes Sense?

This section contains problems from which numerical data has been removed. Children choose from given numbers to fill in the blanks so that the problems and solutions make sense.

Section 2: What's Wrong?

In this section children are given problems to solve. They then compare their solutions with solutions that contain errors in reasoning and use their findings to identify the nature of the errors.

Section 3: What Would You Do?

This section features open-ended problem situations. In each case, children solve the problem based upon their experiences, knowledge of the situation, and individual preference and then support their solutions.

Section 4: What Questions Can You Answer?

This section contains mathematical settings with numerical data. Children generate two questions that can be answered based on the data.

Section 5: What's Missing?

Each problem in this section is missing data required to solve the problem. Children identify what is missing, supply appropriate data, and then solve the problem.

 © Wright Group/McGraw-Hill 0-7622-1347-7

Section 6: What's the Question if You Know the Answer?

This section contains problem situations that include data but no questions. Children are given several possible answers for which they must supply appropriate questions.

How to Use This Book

Each section begins with an extensive teaching lesson that walks children through a problem similar to the rest of the problems in the section. Suggested questions are provided. Responses generated in discussion during the first lesson allow children an opportunity to share their thinking and listen to the thinking of their peers. These discussions help children clarify their understanding of the process for solving the problems in the section.

The other teaching lessons in each section are designed to guide children as they are learning procedures. Depending on the needs of your children, you may wish to teach these as either whole-group or small-group lessons. A great deal of interesting dialogue and thoughtful questioning will result from either format.

The problems in this book can be used in a variety of ways.

Class Opener or Warm up

Present the problem as an opening exercise to involve children in a discussion that can carry over into the day's lesson.

Class Closer

If there are a few minutes left at the end of a class period, introduce a problem in class and assign it as a homework or a family activity. Have children discuss the work at the beginning of the next day.

Small-group or Partners Activity

After you have introduced the first lesson in a section, most children will be able to solve the remaining problems with a partner or in a small group. Working in this way, children can share their thinking with their peers and get important feedback.

Individual Activity

After children have participated in the first lesson in a section and have worked with a partner or small group, some may be ready to solve additional problems individually. The ability to work these problems independently will vary from child to child.

Assessment

Suggested answers to problems in this book can be found at the end of each section. However, you might prefer using a rubric to evaluate children's reasoning. You might even decide to check one section, or certain problems within a section, using the answer key and to assess other sections or problems within a section using a rubric.

A rubric is helpful in assessing a child's mathematical proficiency in relationship to specific criteria. It can be used to evaluate various dimensions of mathematical activity such as problem solving, communication, use of mathematical language, reasoning, and number sense.

© Wright Group/McGraw-Hill 0-7622-1347-7

The following general 3-point rubric can be used with any problem in any section of this book. If you prefer, feel free to develop your own rubric to provide for a more specific assessment. When using a rubric, it is recommended that you discuss the criteria with your children ahead of time. Doing so will help children to understand what a complete response should include and will encourage them to take time to reflect on their answers.

3	The child accomplishes the purpose of the question or task. Understanding of the mathematics in the task is demonstrated, and the child is able to communicate his or her reasoning.
2	The child partially accomplishes the purpose of the question or task. Understanding of the mathematics may not be complete OR the child may not be able to communicate his or her reasoning adequately.
1	The child is not able to accomplish the purpose of the question or task. Understanding of the mathematics is fragmented, and the communication is vague or incomplete.

Section 1 | What Number Makes Sense?

IN THIS SECTION, CHILDREN ARE PRESENTED with problem situations from which numerical data are missing. A set of numbers are provided, and children determine where to place each number so the situation makes sense.

It is suggested that the first problem in this section be used as a whole-class activity.

The procedures outlined in the first problem will help children understand how to

a) carefully read the numerical situation,

b) decide which numbers to place in each blank,

c) determine whether or not the numbers they chose make sense.

The group interaction that occurs during the lesson will provide an opportunity for children to explain their thinking.

Consider having children work the next two problems in the section either with a partner or in a small group. After they have had a chance to become comfortable working with this type of problem, some children may be able to complete the last two problems independently.

As they work through the exercises here, children practice computation and increase their repertoire of problem-solving skills. Reasoning skills are improved by exposing children to a variety of ways to solve a problem. Be sure to engage children in a class discussion after each problem has been completed so they can hear ways of solving problems that differ from their own.

Mathematical Skills
. . . .

Problem 1
Comparing and Ordering Numbers

Problem 2
Counting, Repeated Addition

Problem 3
Counting

Problem 4
Telling Time

Problem 5
Money—Value of Dimes and Nickels, Addition

Teaching Problem 1 | # Happy Birthday, Kayla!

Teaching Goal

As children begin each lesson in this section, they read an incomplete rebus number story. Then they work together to fit the numbers that appear at the bottom of their worksheets into the story to complete it. In this first lesson, children assign numbers to the story to explain that Kayla's sister is 10 years old, her brother is 2 years old, and Kayla herself is 6 years old.

Teaching Plan

1. Present the problem to the class.

2. Read the problem aloud as children follow along.

3. Have children work collaboratively in pairs or in small groups to solve the problem. Point out that there are different ways to go about solving a problem, such as modeling it with manipulatives, acting it out, retelling it (in the child's own words), and by drawing a picture.

4. Lead a whole-group discussion of the problem.

Reading the Problem Aloud

Tell children that they are going to read a story about a girl named Kayla who has a big sister and a little brother. Explain that, to complete the story, children must find how old Kayla is. They do this by first finding out how old her sister and her brother are. Read the title of the problem and the first line of the story aloud.

▶ Have children point to the rebus picture of the girl in item 1. Explain that this is Kayla's "big sister." Ask children to raise their hands if they have a big sister. Elicit the ages of some of the big sisters along with each child's own age. Be sure that everyone understands that each big sister is *older than* the child in the class is.

(continued on page 4)

Materials
....
Scissors
Glue sticks
Birthday candles, 7 per child, pair, or group (optional)

Discuss the Meaning of
....
older
younger
question mark
age

Name
....

Problem 1 **Happy Birthday, Kayla!**

Today is Kayla's birthday.

1. Kayla's big  is ☐ years old.

Her little is ☐ years old.

Kayla is ☐ years old today.

2. Draw candles on Kayla's birthday cake.

 ☐ 2   ☐ 6   ☐ 10

Reading the Problem Aloud *continued*

Now have children point to the rebus picture of the boy. Say that this is Kayla's "little brother." Ask for everyone who has a little brother to raise his or her hand. Elicit the ages of some of the little brothers along with each child's own age. Explain that each little brother is *younger than* the child in the class is.

Have children follow along on their papers as you read the following aloud.

> Kayla's big sister is *how many* years old?
> Her little brother is *how many* years old?
> Kayla is *how many* years old today?

Draw attention to the numbers at the bottom of the worksheet. Have everyone read the numbers together: **"Two, six, ten."** Explain that these numbers tell how old Kayla, her big sister, and her little brother are. Children must put these numbers into the story.

▶ Distribute scissors and guide children in cutting along the dotted lines to separate the numbers. Tell them to decide where to put the numbers on the boxes in the story.

Allow them enough time to manipulate the numbers on the boxes until they are satisfied that they have found the correct placement for each. (Alternatively, you may have children who are able to copy the numbers write them in place on the lines in the story.)

Call on volunteers to read each of the completed sentences in item 1. The story should now be read as:

> Kayla's big sister is 10 years old.
> Her little brother is 2 years old.
> Kayla is 6 years old today.

Now ask, **How did you decide how old Kayla is? How could you tell how old her big sister is? How could you know her little brother's age?**

Once children agree on the correct placement of the cut-out numbers, have them glue the numbers in place.

▶ Now, read item 2 aloud, **"Draw candles on Kayla's birthday cake."** Allow children to first choose the correct number of candles (or small counters to stand for candles) for Kayla's cake. Then have children place the candles on the birthday cake and count to see that they have the correct number before drawing them on the cake.

Ask, **How many candles did you put on the cake?** Children should understand that the cake should have 6 candles, one for each year of Kayla's age.

If none of the children mentions putting still one more candle on the cake, point out that some people put a "good-luck" candle on a birthday cake.

Then ask, **If you put one candle for good luck on Kayla's cake, then how many candles would be on the cake?** Suggest that anyone who would like to draw a good-luck candle on his or her cake may do so.

. . . .

This think-and-check problem-solving process, along with class discussion, allows children to use, extend, and communicate their reasoning and logic skills.

Teaching Problem 2 | # How Many?

Teaching Goal

Tell children that they are going to read a math story about friends who stop the game that they are playing to do some counting.

In this lesson, children assign numbers to identify three people's total numbers of noses, arms, and toes. Then they decide on and record a possible number of smiles for the three people.

Reading the Problem Aloud

Read the title of the problem and the first two sentences aloud. Discuss the *Hokey Pokey* and make sure children understand that this game is played by forming a circle and singing as each player puts an arm, a leg, or another body part into the circle.

Have children point to the rebus pictures in item 1 as you identify each as a *nose,* an *arm,* and *toes.* Tell them to pretend that David, Ann, and Beth are asking some questions. Have the class follow along as you read the questions aloud.

> **All together, we count *how many* noses?**
> **All together, we count *how many* arms?**
> **All together, we count *how many* toes?**

You may wish to call on three children in the class to pretend to be David, Ann, and Beth. Have the class jointly count these children's total number of noses, arms, and toes. At this point, some children will realize that the numbers at the bottom of their worksheets match the totals that they have found. Have children either cut out the numbers and glue them where they belong in the story or refer to the numbers and write them in the story.

Ask children how they know their answers make sense. One way to help them explain is to ask them how many noses, arms, and toes one person has; then how many of each two people have and how many of each three people have.

Then read item 2 aloud. Have children draw the number of smiles three children could have all together.

Materials
....
Scissors
Glue sticks

Discuss the Meaning of
....
How many?
Hokey Pokey

After the Lesson
....
Use these questions as part of a whole-group discussion.

What is the greatest number of smiles that the three children could have? What is the least number of smiles?

If one more child joins David, Ann, and Beth, then how many noses would there be? How many arms? How many toes?

Name
....

Problem 2 **How Many?**

David, Ann, and Beth do the Hokey Pokey.
They stop to count.

1. All together, we count  .

All together, we count  .

All together, we count .

2. Draw how many  they have all together.

$$ 3 \quad 6 \quad 30 $$

Teaching Problem 3 | # On the Farm

Teaching Goal

Tell children that they are going to read a math story about some animals that live on a farm.

In this lesson, children assign numbers to identify how many farm animals are pictured and the total number of each kind of animal. They use counters to show the number of each and then record the numbers on their worksheets.

Reading the Problem Aloud

Read the title of the problem and the first sentence of the story aloud. Discuss the kinds of animals that may live on a farm. Then say that a small farm may have just a few animals, like the ones children see at the top of their worksheets. Elicit the names of these animals, but do not discuss their numbers.

Have children point to the rebus pictures in item 1 as you identify the animals as a *sheep*, a *duck*, and a *cow*. Then read the following aloud as children follow along.

> There are *how many* sheep?
> There are *how many* ducks?
> There are *how many* cows?

If animal counters that match the kinds of animals shown are available, distribute them. Alternatively, distribute counters of three colors that children can use to model the animals at the top of the page.

At this point, some children will realize that the numbers at the bottom of their worksheets match the numbers of animals that they have modeled. Have children either cut out these numbers and glue them where they belong in the story, or have children copy and write the numbers in place in the story.

Read item 2 aloud. Ask children to arrange all nine of their counters on the grass. Some may wish to draw the animals on the grass to record their numbers.

Materials
....
Scissors
Glue sticks
Animal counters
(optional)

Discuss the Meaning of
....
closer together
farther apart

After the Lesson
....
Use these questions as part of a whole-group discussion.

How did you put your animals on the grass? Are all the sheep together, or are they with the ducks and the cow?

If you moved all your animals closer together (or "farther apart"), would there be fewer animals (or "more animals")? Some children may need to move their animals and recount them in each position to confirm that their numbers remain constant regardless of their positions.

Problem 3 **On the Farm**

Count the animals on the farm.

1. There are [ ]  .

There are [ ]  .

There is just [ ] 🐄 .

2. Use counters for animals. Put them on the grass.

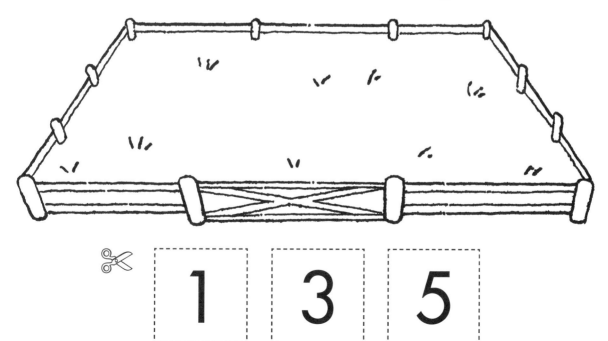

✂ | 1 | 3 | 5 |

Teaching Problem 4 | # Watch the Clock

Teaching Goal

Tell children that they are going to read a math story about a boy who looks at a clock many times each day.

In this lesson, children assign numbers to identify the times at which a boy named John goes to school, eats lunch, and plays baseball. Then they decide on a bedtime for John and draw hands in the correct positions on a clockface to record that time.

Reading the Problem Aloud

Read the title of the problem and the first sentence of the story aloud. Discuss with children what it means to be "on time." Explain that to be on time for school, John must be there when the clock shows the time for the school day to start. If he gets there before that time, then he is *early*. If he gets there after that time, then he is *late*.

Have children point to the rebus pictures in item 1 as you identify them as *John's school, John eating lunch,* and *John playing baseball.* Have the class follow along as you read about John's day this way.

> **He goes to school at** *what time?*
> **He eats lunch at** *what time?*
> **He plays baseball at** *what time?*

Draw children's attention to the numbers at the bottom of their worksheets. Tell them that each of these numbers stands for the time that one of John's activities begins. Call on volunteers to name the time at which John goes to school (8 o'clock), eats lunch (12 o'clock), and plays baseball (4 o'clock). Display a large clock and have a volunteer move the clock hands to show each time. Have children either cut out the numbers and glue them where they belong in the story, or have children copy and write the numbers in the story.

Read item 2 aloud. Have the class vote to decide on John's bedtime. Model the agreed-to time on the clock. (If children decide on a time such as 7:30, elicit that this time is between two hours—in this case, between 7 and 8.)

Materials
....
Scissors
Glue sticks
"Clockworks" clock
(or other clock
with movable hands)
(optional)

Discuss the Meaning of
....
on time
early
late
o'clock

After the Lesson
....
Use these questions
as part of a whole-group
discussion.

At what time in the
morning does our school
day begin? Are you
always on time for
school? Have you ever
been early (or late)?

At what time do *you* eat
supper? At what time do
you do your homework?
At what time do *you*
watch TV?

Problem 4 **Watch the Clock**

John is always on time.

1. He goes to at [   ] o'clock.

He at [   ] o'clock.

He at [   ] o'clock.

2. What time do you think John goes to bed?

Draw hands on the clock to show the time.

✂ [**12**] [**8**] [**4**]

Teaching Problem 5 | # Jeremy's Money

Teaching Goal

Tell children that they are going to read a math story about a boy who needs them to help him count his money.

In this lesson, children assign numbers that identify how many coins of each kind are pictured and the total value of each kind. Then they determine the total number of coins pictured and model that number with play money and/or by drawing coins.

Reading the Problem Aloud

Read the title of the problem and the first sentence aloud. Have children point to the two rebus pictures in item 1 as you identify them as *dimes* and as *nickels*. Point out that the equals sign means "has the same value as" or "are worth." Tell children to follow along as you read about Jeremy's money:

> **He has *how many* dimes?**
> **His dimes are worth *how many* cents?**

> **He has *how many* nickels?**
> **His nickels are worth *how many* cents?**

If play money is available, allow children to model Jeremy's money. Alternatively, display actual coins (3 dimes and 3 nickels), and have children count—first the number and value of 1 dime, then of 2 dimes, then of 3 dimes. Repeat this process with 1, 2, and 3 nickels. Record these values on the board.

Some children will realize that the numbers at the bottom of their worksheets match the values that they have found. They may then cut out the numbers at the bottom of the page and glue them into the story or copy and write the numbers in the story.

Read item 2 aloud. Draw two circles on the board—a small circle marked "10¢" and a slightly larger circle marked "5¢." You may have children place their play money on the "hand" on their worksheet to show Jeremy's coins and/or have them draw the coins on the hand.

Materials
....
Scissors
Glue sticks
Play money (dimes and nickels) *or* actual dimes and nickels (optional)

Discuss the Meaning of
....
How many?
worth

After the Lesson
....
Use these questions as part of a whole-group discussion.

What is the total value of Jeremy's coins?

Which is worth more, 1 dime or 1 nickel? 3 dimes or 2 nickels? 2 dimes or 3 nickels?

Suppose Jeremy's sister has 5 coins. Does she have the same amount of money as Jeremy?
She may or may not have the same amount. There are many combinations of 5 coins that she could have.

Name
....

Problem 5 **Jeremy's Money**

Jeremy counts his money.

1. He has   .

His  = ¢ .

He has    .

His    =  ¢ .

2. How many coins does
Jeremy have in all?
Draw them in his hand.

✂ | **2** | **3** | **10** | **30** |

Answer Key

Problem 1: Happy Birthday, Kayla!

1. Kayla's big sister is <u>10</u> years old.
   Her little brother is <u>2</u> years old.
   Kayla is <u>6</u> years old today.

2. Children should draw 6 candles on Kayla's cake. They may also draw one "good-luck" candle.

Problem 2: How Many?

1. All together, we count <u>3</u> noses.
   All together, we count <u>6</u> arms.
   All together, we count <u>30</u> toes.

2. Children should draw 3 smiles if they assume that all the children are smiling. Discuss any alternative solutions as children express their strategies and reasoning for them.

Problem 3: On the Farm

1. There are <u>3</u> sheep.
   There are <u>5</u> ducks.
   There is just <u>1</u> cow.

2. Answers will vary. Discuss the solutions as children express their strategies and reasoning for them.

Problem 4: Watch the Clock

1. He goes to school at <u>8</u> o'clock.
   He eats lunch at <u>12</u> o'clock.
   He plays ball at <u>4</u> o'clock.

2. Answers will vary. Discuss the solutions as children express their strategies and reasoning for them.

Problem 5: Jeremy's Money

1. He has <u>3</u> dimes.
   His 3 dimes equal <u>30</u>¢.
   (*or* His three dimes are worth 30¢.)
   He has <u>2</u> nickels.
   His 2 nickels equal <u>10</u>¢.
   (*or* His two nickels are worth 10¢.)

2. Children should draw 3 dimes and 2 nickels. Discuss any alternative solutions as children express their strategies and reasoning for them.

Assessment Note

Children's work on any of the problems in this section can be assessed using the 3-point rubric on page ix.

Section 2   **What's Wrong?**

AFTER CHILDREN SOLVE EACH PROBLEM in this section, they are faced with an alternate, but incorrect solution. An error has been made either in concept, interpretation, or computation. Children use their own experiences in solving to identify the error that was made in the alternate solution.

It is recommended that the first problem in this section be used as a whole-class activity.

The procedures outlined in the first problem will take children through the process of

a) finding the correct solution to the problem,

b) identifying the error that was made.

Consider having children work the next two problems in the section either with a partner or in a small group. This will provide an opportunity for them to become comfortable working with this type of problem. The last two problems may then be assigned to some children to complete independently.

This section deals with error analysis. Each exercise offers an effective means for children to practice computation skills within a problem-solving context. Different strategies such as drawing diagrams or pictures, writing an equation, or creating a table or graph may be used to solve problems. By engaging in class discussion after a problem has been completed, children will be able to hear ways of solving problems that differ from their own. The group interaction that occurs during these discussions often leads to deeper mathematical understanding.

Teaching Problem 1 | # Action Figures

Materials

....

Counters: 20 per child—
10 of each of two colors

Discuss the Meaning of

....

gave

more

first

Teaching Goal

As children participate in each lesson in this section, they work together to identify what the character in the math story did that was wrong. In this first lesson, Lena mistakenly believes that if she starts out with 10 action figures and then gets 4 more, she will end up with 6 action figures—fewer than she had before. The error is that Lena *took away* 4 action figures from her 10. Instead, she should have *added* 4 to her 10. Children should understand that we use addition to show that an amount has increased.

Teaching Plan

1. Present the problem to the class.

2. Read the problem aloud as children follow along.

3. Have children work collaboratively in pairs or in small groups to solve the problem. Point out that there are different ways to go about solving a problem, such as modeling it with manipulatives, acting it out, retelling it (in the child's own words), and by drawing a picture.

4. Lead a whole-group discussion of the problem.

Reading the Problem Aloud

Tell children that they are going to read a number story about a girl named Lena who collects action figures.

Read the title of the problem aloud. Ask children to point to the "toys" across the middle of the page. Explain that these are action figures. Tell children that the pictures of these figures will help them read the story at the top of the page along with you. Have them follow along on their papers as you read the following aloud.

(continued on page 18)

Name
....

Problem 1 **Action Figures**

Lena had 10 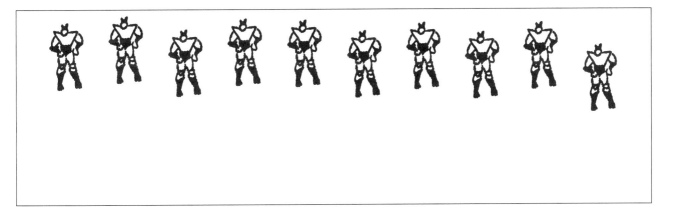.

Mike gave her 4 more .

How many does Lena have now?

1. Lena started with these. Show what happened next.

2. How many does Lena have now? _____

3. This is what Lena thinks.

$$10 - 4 = 6$$

4. Tell what Lena did that was wrong.

Reading the Problem Aloud continued

> Lena had 10 action figures.
> Mike gave her 4 more action figures.
> How many action figures does Lena have now?

▶ Read the first part of item 1 aloud, **"Lena started with these."** Allow time for children to determine how many action figures appear in the box.

Tell children to point to the "first" figure in the row. Then tell them to point to each one of the other figures in this row as you count them together. Remind children that these 10 figures are the ones that Lena "started with."

▶ Read the second part of item 1 aloud, **"Show what happened next."** At this point, you may wish to allow children to model the problem with counters of two colors.

Tell children to take enough counters of one color to stand for the 10 figures that Lena started with and to take enough counters of the other color to stand for the 4 figures that Mike gave her. Suggest that they think about how they could record, or write, what happened next. (They may choose to draw four more figures or to write the expression "10 + 4.")

Ask, **After Mike gives Lena 4 more figures, will she have more figures than she had at first or fewer figures than she had at first?** (She will have *more* figures than she had at first.)

▶ Tell children to follow along as you read item 2 aloud, **"How many action figures does Lena have now?"** Point out that "now" means *after* Mike gave her 4 figures. Elicit that Lena now has a total of 14 action figures. Children may choose to write "14" or the number sentence "10 + 4 = 14.")

Write the number sentence on the board and read it aloud as, **"10 plus 4 equals 14."**

Ask, **How can you check to be sure that Lena now has 14 action figures?** (Accept all reasonable answers. Additionally, you may wish to have children count on from 10, "…11, 12, 13, 14," as they point, one by one, either to the pictured action figures or to their counters.)

▶ Read item 3 aloud, **"This is what Lena thinks. Ten take away four equals six."** Write the number sentence "$10 - 4 = 6$" on the board and have children point to it on their papers. Children should understand that the girl in the picture is Lena and that 6 is the number of action figures that Lena thinks she has now.

Ask, **Is Lena's answer to the problem like yours in any way?** (Some of the numbers in the number sentences are the same.)

How is your answer different from Lena's? (Lena's answer is 6. Also, Lena's number sentence has a minus sign, not a plus sign.)

▶ Read item 4 aloud, **"Tell what Lena did that was wrong."** Lead a discussion about this question. Children should be able to say that Lena was thinking about taking away, or subtracting, the 4 figures Mike gave her from the 10 she started with. She should not have subtracted. Instead, she should have added the 4 figures to the 10 she started with. (Explain that this is why there is a plus sign in the number sentence that correctly tells the math story, $10 + 4 = 14$.)

....

Note that there are several possible reasons for which a child like Lena might choose to subtract, instead of add, to solve this problem. For example, she might think of the key word *gave* as signaling the operation of subtraction, she might confuse the roles of the characters in the story, or she might think that subtracting a smaller number from a larger one yields a number that is actually greater than either of the others.

You may wish to encourage children to use a specific representation to solve the different problems in this section. You may also have them try to use multiple representations, such as a drawing and writing a number sentence, to solve one or more of the problems.

Teaching Problem 2 | **Fly Away**

Materials (optional)
....
10 counters per child

Discuss the Meaning of
....
fly away
left in the tree

After the Lesson
....
Use these questions
as part of a whole-group
discussion.

**If there are 7 birds in the
tree and then 2 birds fly
away, will there be more
birds or fewer birds left
in the tree?** There will be
fewer birds.

**How can you check
to be sure that 5 birds
were left in the tree?**
Answers will vary.

**What number sentence
tells this story?**
7 − 2 = 5

Teaching Goal

Tell children that they are going to read a math story about the birds that a girl named Taylor saw in a tree.

In this lesson, Taylor mistakenly believes that if there were 7 birds in the tree and then 2 flew away, 9 birds would be left in the tree—more birds than there were at first. The error is that Taylor *added* 2 birds to the 7. Instead, she should have *subtracted* 2 from the 7. Children should understand that we use subtraction to show that an amount has decreased.

Reading the Problem Aloud

Read the title of the problem aloud. Write "7" and "2" on the board. Ask children to find these numbers in the sentences near the top of the page and to point to them. Explain that in this story 7 and 2 stand for numbers of birds. Read the following aloud.

> **Taylor saw 7 birds in a tree.**
> **She saw 2 birds fly away.**
> **How many birds were left in the tree?**

Read item 1 aloud. At this point, allow children to select counters to model the birds that Taylor saw in the tree. Suggest that they then "take away" counters to model the birds that fly away.

Read items 2–4 aloud, one at a time, stopping in between to help children respond, to explain what Taylor thinks is the answer to the problem, and to compare their answer to Taylor's.

In response to item 4, children should be able to say that what Taylor did that was wrong was to add instead of subtract.

Problem 2 **Fly Away**

Taylor saw 7 🐦 in a tree.

She saw 2 🐦 fly away.

How many 🐦 were left in the tree?

1. Taylor saw these. Show what happened when 2 flew away.

🐦   🐦   🐦   🐦   🐦   🐦   🐦

2. How many 🐦 were left in the tree? _____

3. This is what Taylor thinks.

$7 + 2 = 9$

4. Tell what Taylor did that was wrong.

Teaching Problem 3 | # Finger Puppets

Teaching Goal

Tell children that they are going to read a math story about a boy's three animal finger puppets. The animals are a zebra, a monkey, and a giraffe.

In this lesson, Dan mistakenly believes that there are just three possible arrangements of the three finger puppets. Children should determine that there are six possible arrangements.

Reading the Problem Aloud

Read the title of the problem aloud. Draw children's attention to the three finger puppets shown at the top of the page. Explain that in this story they will figure out different ways to line up three puppets. Read the following aloud.

> **Dan has three finger puppets.**
> **He puts them on his fingers.**
> **How many ways can he do this?**

Read item 1 aloud, **"Cut out the finger puppets at the bottom of the page. Show different ways to line them up."** Have children cut out the puppets at the bottom of the page and glue them onto stickies. Then have them stick the puppets onto their fingers. Alternatively, have children select counters of three colors to model the puppets.

Allow sufficient time for children to work with the puppets. Then read item 2. Ask volunteers to name the different ways of arranging the puppets. Make a list of children's suggestions, perhaps sketching the sequence of animal faces for each suggestion.

Read items 3–4. Have volunteers model Dan's ways of arranging the puppets. In a discussion, children should be able to say that what Dan did "wrong" was to think that there are only three ways to arrange the puppets. Encourage them to identify the (three) ways that Dan did *not* find. They can do this by comparing Dan's three ways to the class's list of six ways.

Materials
....
Scissors
Glue stick
Sticky notes
Counters (optional)

Discuss the Meaning of
....
finger puppets
arrangement

After the Lesson
....
Use these questions as part of a whole-group discussion.

How many ways can Dan put the puppets on his fingers if the zebra comes first? 2 ways

How many ways can Dan put the puppets on his fingers if the zebra comes first and the monkey comes second? 1 way

Problem 3 **Finger Puppets**

Dan has 3 .

He puts them on his  .

How many ways can he do this?

1. Cut out the  . Show different ways to line them up.

2. How many ways are there?_____

3. This is what Dan thinks.

4. Tell what Dan did that was wrong.

Teaching Problem 4 | # Rock Turtles

Teaching Goal

Tell children that they are going to read a math story about the rock turtles that a boy makes from rocks and paper clips.

In this lesson, Jackson mistakenly thinks that he can make 10 rock turtles from his 10 rocks and 25 paper clips. Children will determine that Jackson has only enough materials to make 5 turtles.

Reading the Problem Aloud

Read the title of the problem aloud. Have children look at the "rock turtle" at the top of the page. Be sure they understand that it is made from 1 rock and 5 paper clips—with one clip for the head and 4 clips for each of the legs. Have children follow along as you read this aloud.

> **Jackson made a rock turtle.**
> **He used 1 rock and 5 paper clips.**
> **How many rock turtles can he make with 10 rocks and 25 paper clips?**

Read item 1 aloud. Have children, working in pairs, cut out the 10 "rocks" from one worksheet. Distribute 25 paper clips to each pair. Tell them to make as many rock turtles as they can with their materials. (Alternatively, you may have children use actual rocks for the turtle bodies and counters for the extremities.)

Read item 2 aloud. Develop a chart with the following headings to help children determine that it is possible to make 5 rock turtles from the given materials.

Number of Turtles	Number of Rocks	Number of Paper clips
1	1	5

Read items 3–4. In a discussion, children should be able to say that Jackson was "wrong" when he thought that he could make 10 turtles. Even though Jackson had enough rocks for 10 turtles, he did not have enough paper clips.

Materials
....
Scissors
Paper clips
Small rocks or small
square or rectangular
blocks and
Counters (optional)

Discuss the Meaning of
....
rock turtle
paper clip
enough

After the Lesson
....
Use these questions
as part of a whole-group
discussion.

After Jackson makes his turtles, how many rocks will he have left over?
5 rocks

How many paper clips would Jackson need to make 10 turtles?
50 paperclips

How many more paper clips would Jackson need to get in order to have enough for 10 turtles? 25 more

Problem 4 **Rock Turtles**

Jackson made a .

He used 1 ⬭ and 5 ⬭.

How many can he make with 10 ⬭ and 25 ⬭?

1. Cut out the 10 ⬭. Get 25 ⬭.

2. How many 🐢 can he make? _____

3. This is what Jackson thinks.

I can make 10.

4. Tell what Jackson did that was wrong.

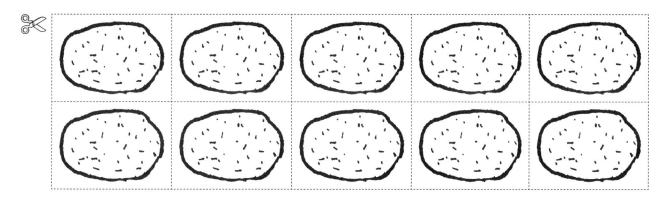

Teaching Problem 5 | # Shape Pattern

Materials (optional)

....

Attribute Blocks (squares and triangles, each in two sizes) or Counters (of two kinds, each in two sizes)

Discuss the Meaning of

....

pattern
square
triangle
repeat

After the Lesson

....

Use these questions as part of a whole-group discussion.

How are the shapes in the pattern alike? How are they different?

Now you know that the little triangle comes next. So, what should come next, *after* the little triangle? a big square

Teaching Goal

Tell children that they are going to read about a pattern that a girl is making from two kinds of shapes of two sizes.

In this lesson, Eva mistakenly believes that a big square should be the next shape in her pattern when, in fact, a little triangle should come next in the pattern.

Reading the Problem Aloud

Read the title of the problem and the first line of the story aloud. Explain that the shapes across the top of the page form a pattern. Elicit that the shapes that make up the pattern are squares and triangles. Encourage children to use their own words to tell how the shapes are arranged in the pattern. They should understand that the core of the pattern is made up of a big square and two little squares followed by a big triangle and two little triangles. Point out that the same shapes repeat on and on in this order to form a pattern. Read aloud, **"What comes next?"**

Have children point to the dotted rule at the right of the pattern. Be sure they understand that they need to figure out which shape—square or triangle—of which size—big or little—belongs in this spot.

Read item 1 aloud, **"Cut out the shapes at the bottom of the page. Try each one at the end of the pattern."** Have children, working in pairs, see how each of their cutouts looks at the end of the pattern.

Read question item 2 aloud, **"Which shape should come next?"** Instead of having children cut out the shapes, or in addition to it, you may wish to have them copy the pattern shown with manipulatives. Then again ask, **What comes next? Should that shape be big or little?** (Children should hold up the manipulative of the appropriate size and shape to show their choice of response.)

Read items 3–4. In a discussion, children should say that Eva is "wrong" because a little triangle, and not a big square, must come next to continue the pattern.

Name

....

Problem 5 **Shape Pattern**

Eva is making this pattern.

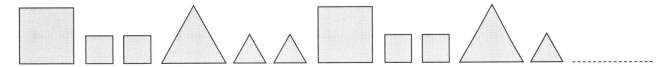

What comes next?

1. Cut out the shapes at the bottom.
Try each one at the end of the pattern.

2. Which shape should come next?

3. This is what Eva thinks.

The big square comes next.

4. Tell what Eva did that was wrong.

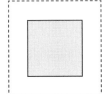
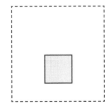
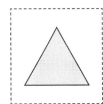

Answer Key

Problem 1: Action Figures

1. Children may choose to draw four more action figures or write the expression "10 + 4."

2. 14

3. Lena thinks "Ten take away four equals six."

4. Lena mistakenly subtracted. She should have added.

Problem 2: Fly Away

1. Children may choose to cross out two birds or write the expression "7 − 2."

2. 5

3. Taylor thinks "Seven plus two equals nine."

4. Taylor mistakenly added. She should have subtracted.

Problem 3: Finger Puppets

1. The puppets can be lined up on three fingers in these six ways:

   zebra — monkey — giraffe
   zebra — giraffe — monkey
   monkey — zebra — giraffe
   monkey — giraffe — zebra
   giraffe — zebra — monkey
   giraffe — monkey — zebra

2. 6

3. Dan mistakenly thinks that there are just three ways to arrange the puppets on his fingers.

4. Dan did not find these three ways of arranging the puppets:

   zebra — giraffe — monkey
   monkey — zebra — giraffe
   giraffe — zebra — monkey

Problem 4: Rock Turtles

1. Children make rock turtles from 10 rocks and 25 paper clips. Each turtle should be made up of 1 rock and 5 paper clips.

2. 5

3. Jackson mistakenly thinks that because he has ten rocks he can make ten turtles.

4. Jackson can make only five turtles because he has 25 paper clips and needs five paper clips for each turtle.

Problem 5: Shape Pattern

1. Children position each of their cut-out shapes at the end of the pattern to determine which one of them "comes next."

2. the little triangle

3. Eva mistakenly thinks that the big square should come next.

4. Eva did not notice that the core of the pattern is made up of a big square and two little squares followed by a big triangle and two little triangles.

Assessment Note

Children's work on any of the problems in this section can be assessed using the 3-point rubric on page ix.

Section 3 What Would You Do?

OPEN-ENDED PROBLEMS ARE PRESENTED in this section. In each case, after finding an answer, children are asked to support their solution.

These problems give children the opportunity to use their prior knowledge as a foundation on which to build and strengthen their skills. Both computation and problem-solving abilities are engaged.

Consider teaching the first problem in this section as a whole-class activity. The next two problems might then be solved within small groups with the last two problems completed by some children working independently.

Group discussions about solutions provide an important forum for a valuable exchange of ideas. These discussions allow children to practice effective communication of their own mathematical thinking and to gain insights and understanding through listening to the solution strategies of others.

Mathematical Skills
....

Problem 1
Counting, Addition, Subtraction, Grouping

Problem 2
Number Sense, Equal Units, Counting, Combinations

Problem 3
Sorting, Classifying, Geometry

Problem 4
Place Value

Problem 5
Interpreting Data, Ordering, Ordinal Numbers

Teaching Problem 1 | **Class Pets**

Teaching Goal

As children participate in each lesson in this section, they work together to determine how a given number of items can be sorted, or otherwise arranged, according to a given situation. In this first lesson, children decide on ways in which 7 goldfish can be put into 3 bowls.

Teaching Plan

1. Present the problem to the class.

2. Read the problem aloud as children follow along.

3. Have children work collaboratively in pairs or in small groups to solve the problem. Point out that there are different ways to go about solving a problem, such as modeling it with manipulatives, acting it out, retelling it (in the child's own words), and by drawing a picture.

4. Lead a whole-group discussion of the problem.

Reading the Problem Aloud

Tell children that they are going to read a number story about a boy named Pedro who has 7 goldfish in his classroom.

▶ Read the title of the problem aloud and tell children to point to each picture of a goldfish as you read the following aloud.

> Pedro's class has 7 goldfish.
> Help Pedro put them into 3 bowls.
> Each bowl must have at least 1 goldfish.
> No bowl may have more than 3 goldfish.
> How many fish would you put into each bowl?

(continued on page 32)

Name
....

Problem 1 **Class Pets**

Pedro's class has 7  .

Help Pedro put them into 3 bowls.

Each bowl must have at least 1  .

No bowl may have more than 3  .

How many fish would you put into each bowl?

Reading the Problem Aloud *continued*

► Explain that children will use counters as goldfish and then show how many of these goldfish they can put into each fishbowl. (If some children are ready to offer answers without using counters at this point, allow them to draw goldfish in the bowls to show their answers.)

Make counters available. Tell children to take the correct number of counters (7) to stand for the total number of goldfish in Pedro's classroom. Allow sufficient time for children to move the "goldfish" from one "bowl" to the next. When they are satisfied with the way the fish are arranged, have them draw the number of fish in each bowl.

Note that some children will need help in one-to-one matching; that is, in drawing one goldfish to represent one counter. Help them do this by telling them to take one counter out of a bowl with their non-drawing hand and to hold it while they draw a fish in its place in the bowl with their drawing hand. After the drawing is done, that counter should be put off to the side of the desk. The next counter should be taken out of the bowl and held in one hand while another goldfish is drawn in the bowl, and so on.

► When children have completed their work ask, **Have you put all 7 goldfish into bowls? Have you put at least 1 fish into all 3 bowls?**

Children may assign the 7 goldfish to the 3 bowls in either of these ways:

2 bowls have 3 goldfish each, and 1 bowl has 1 goldfish.

2 bowls have 2 goldfish each, and 1 bowl has 3 goldfish.

▶ Finally ask, **How did you decide where to put each goldfish?**
Accept any reasonable responses to this question. For example,
even though all the actual goldfish may be presumed to be one
color, children who are working with counters of more than one
color may say that they decided to put their "fish" of one color into
one bowl and their "fish" of other colors into the other bowls.
Alternatively, children may say that they would put the smallest
fish into the first bowl, the medium-size fish into the second bowl,
and the biggest fish into the third bowl.

If an incorrect solution is suggested, such as "4 goldfish in one
bowl" or "1 bowl with no goldfish," ask children how they
can tell whether the solution is correct. To do so, reread the initial
conditions of the problem and ask if each one has been met.

....

Since the problems in this section are somewhat open-ended, there
may be a variety of strategies and solutions. It is important to
encourage the children to choose a solution that they can defend.

Teaching Problem 2 | # Pizza Toppings

Teaching Goal

Tell children that they are going to read a math story about a pizza that has been cut into 4 slices that are all the same size.

In this lesson, children will read that 3 toppings must be put on 4 slices of pizza. They must determine how each topping could be put on the given number of slices and conclude that some slices will have more than one topping.

Reading the Problem Aloud

Read the title of the problem and the first line of the story aloud. Write "1 slice," "2 slices," and "3 slices" on the board. Read the words aloud, having children repeat them after you. Now have children point to the pictures of the pizza toppings—mushroom, pepperoni, and cheese—on their worksheets. Tell children to "read" the sentences along with you as you read them aloud.

> **She must put mushrooms on 1 slice.**
> **She must put pepperoni on 2 slices.**
> **She must put cheese on 3 slices.**

Now read, **"Show where Mrs. Ford could put the toppings."** Explain that the picture shows how a pizza would look on a table. The lines on the pizza show where it was cut. Draw a pizza with lines on the board. Lead the class in counting the four slices in unison.

Have children select counters to model the three toppings. You may wish to designate brown counters as "mushroom slices," red counters as "pepperoni," and yellow counters as "cheese." Then give children enough time to figure out how to place the toppings.

Some children may infer that Mrs. Ford needs 6 slices for 6 toppings and may protest that 4 slices are not enough. If this happens, assure children that 4 slices *is* enough. Elicit that they must think about how they can put *more than just one topping* on some slices.

After completing their work and discussing the after-the-lesson questions, children may draw their solutions on their pizza slices.

Materials (optional)
....
Counters of three colors

Discuss the Meaning of
....
pizza toppings
pepperoni

After the Lesson
....
Use these questions as part of a whole-group discussion.

On which slice did you put mushrooms? Did you put other toppings on that slice too?

On how many slices did you put cheese? Did you also put other toppings on any of these slices? If so, which ones?

Do you think that there are any other ways to solve this problem? (Have children walk around the classroom to see how their work compares with the work of others.)

Problem 2 **Pizza Toppings**

Help Mrs. Ford make pizza for 4.

She must put 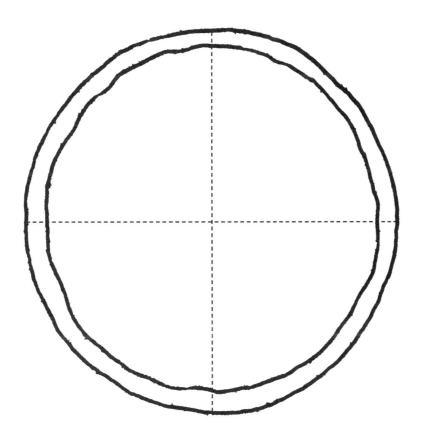 on 1 slice.

She must put on 2 slices.

She must put on 3 slices.

Show where Mrs. Ford could put the toppings.

Teaching Problem 3 | # Shape Sort

Teaching Goal

Tell children that they are going to read a math story about a girl who needs their help in sorting a group of cards with shapes on them.

In this lesson, children will sort 12 geometric figures according to the attributes of their choosing, such as shape, shading, and orientation.

Reading the Problem Aloud

Read aloud the title of the problem, and then have children look at the cards at the bottom of the worksheet. Call on children to identify the shapes on the cards. In addition to naming each shape as a rectangle, triangle, or square and identifying it as being open (or white), shaded, or striped, children may allude to specific figures by using ordinal numbers. That is, they may refer to the *first, second, third,* or *fourth* figure in each of the three rows. As each shape is identified, ask everyone to point to it on his or her worksheet. If a child's description of a shape is not succinct enough for others to identify it, ask, **What else can you tell us about that shape?**

Have pairs of children work together to cut out one set of the 12 cards. Then have them sort the shapes *in any way they like.* Compare the ways that children sorted. Then read the following aloud:

> **Debra has 12 cards with shapes on them.**
> **Help her sort them into 3 piles.**

Now tell children to sort their shapes so that they have three piles. Pay special attention to the way in which children sort the squares since the squares appear in two different orientations. Some children may fail to recognize that a shape remains the same when it is rotated, or turned.

Materials

Scissors

Discuss the Meaning of

sort
first, second, third, fourth

After the Lesson

Use these questions as part of a whole-group discussion.

How did you make your three piles? (Possibilities include: open figures, shaded figures, and striped figures; rectangles, squares, and triangles; and grouping according to the rows in which the figures appeared before they were cut apart.)

Do each of your piles have the same number of shapes?

How many shapes do you have in each of your piles?

Could you make a different set of three piles? Explain.

Problem 3 **Shape Sort**

Debra has 12 cards with shapes on them.

Help her sort them into 3 piles.

Cut out the cards.

Sort them.

✂

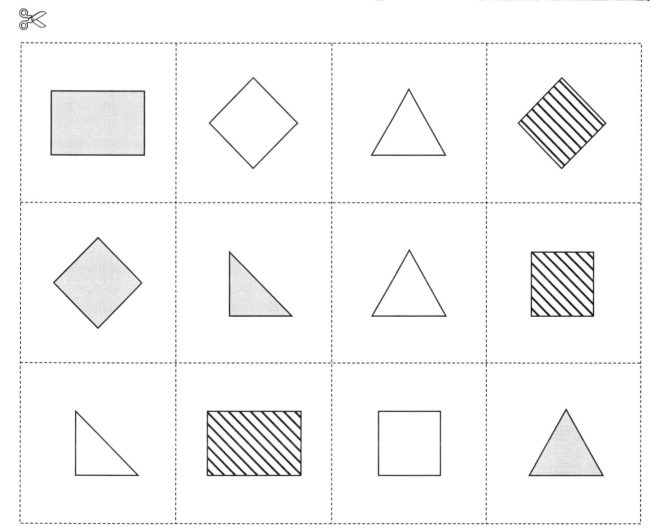

Teaching Problem 4 | # Mystery Number

Teaching Goal

Tell children that they are going to read a math story about a mystery number.

In this lesson, children will read that Brad is thinking of a number with a "6" in it. The children's challenge is to represent any number of their choosing that fits this single condition.

Reading the Problem Aloud

Read the title of the problem aloud. Ask children why any problem might be called a "mystery." Acknowledge their responses. Explain that in this lesson Brad's number is a "mystery" because we do not know what his number is, but we can make some guesses about it.

Write a big "6" on the board. Have children point to the "6" in the story. Ask them to follow along as you read the first three lines aloud.

> **Brad is thinking of a number.**
> **The number has a "6" in it.**
> **What could Brad's number be?**

Children should infer that the picture shows Brad thinking of his number. He could also be thinking, "I know my number. Now you find it!"

Now read, **"Tell or show what Brad's number could be."**

Allow children to decide how to show their numbers. They may represent them with base-ten blocks or counters that they place on their worksheets. They may write their numbers, or they may ask you to record a number that they dictate to you.

It is likely that some children will identify "6" itself as the mystery number. Most will name 2-digit numbers, such as 16, 36, or 67. A few will name, or attempt to write, numbers made up of three or more digits. All legitimate numbers should be accepted.

Materials (optional)

Base-ten blocks or Counters

Discuss the Meaning of

number
digit
question mark

After the Lesson

Use these questions as part of a whole-group discussion.

What could Brad's number be if it starts with 6 and has two digits?

If Brad's number has two digits and ends with 6, what could it be?

If Brad's number has three digits and 6 is the middle digit, what could the number be?

We know that 8 = 6 + 2. Do you think Brad's number could be 8?

Name
....

Problem 4 **Mystery Number**

Brad is thinking of a number.

The number has a "6" in it.

What could Brad's number be?

Tell or show what Brad's number could be.

[blank answer box]

Teaching Problem 5 | # Ready, Set, Go!

Teaching Goal

Tell children that they are going to read a math story about a relay race.

In this lesson, children will decide on the order in which four children will run in a relay race. They may make their decisions based on the age and/or gender of the runners or on any other reasonable criteria.

Reading the Problem Aloud

Read the title of the problem aloud. Ask children to tell when they might have said or heard the words "Ready, set, go!" Explain that two or more teams run in a relay race. The runners on each team line up, one behind the other. As soon as someone says "Ready, set, go!" the first runner on each team runs up to a goal and then runs back to touch the hand of the second runner. Then the second runner runs up to the goal and runs back to touch the hand of the third runner, and so on. The team whose last runner finishes first wins the race.

Read the first two lines of the story aloud:

> **Get ready for the relay race.**
> **Decide who will run first, second, third, and fourth.**

Call on volunteers to read the names and ages of the children in the pictures. Now read, **"Show how the children will run."** Point out that the numbers at the bottom of the worksheet stand for first, second, third, and fourth positions. Explain that in this race a runner who is in the fourth position is also "last." After children decide on the positions for the four runners, they may copy the runners' names above the corresponding positions or they may try to draw pictures of them in each position.

Finally, call on four children to act the parts of the runners. Call on others to name the positions they chose for the race. Ask them to tell why they decided on the order they chose. Then have the actors arrange themselves to show each set of positions named.

Discuss the Meaning of
....

relay race
first, second, third, fourth
last

After the Lesson
....

Use these questions as part of a whole-group discussion.

Suppose another runner joins the team as captain. Then:

Who would you have run first?

Who would you have run in each of the other places?

How many places would there be? 5

Name
....

Problem 5 **Ready, Set, Go!**

Get ready for the relay race.

Decide who will run first, second, third, and fourth.

Show how the children will run.

| **1** | **2** | **3** | **4** |
| First | Second | Third | Fourth |

Answer Key

Problems 1: Class Pets
Children may either put
3 goldfish into each of two bowls
and 1 goldfish into one bowl or
2 goldfish into each of two bowls
and 3 goldfish into one bowl.

Problem 2: Pizza Toppings
There are many ways in which
children can arrange the three toppings on the given numbers of
slices. (They must first realize that
they will have to put more than
one topping on some slices.)

Problem 3: Shape Sort
Accept any reasonable ways of
making the three piles of shape
cards. Three piles can be made
from the cards with shapes that are
open, shaded, and striped; with
shapes that are rectangles, squares,
and triangles; and with shapes
that reflect the three rows in which
they appeared before they were
cut apart.

Problem 4: Mystery Number
The "mystery number" is any
number that children name in
which the digit 6 appears in any
place-value position.

Problem 5: Ready, Set, Go!
There are 24 possible ways in
which the four children can run
in the four positions.

1st	2nd	3rd	4th
Matt	Sofia	Julio	Erica
Matt	Sofia	Erica	Julio
Matt	Julio	Sofia	Erica
Matt	Julio	Erica	Sofia
Matt	Erica	Sofia	Julio
Matt	Erica	Julio	Sofia
Sofia	Julio	Erica	Matt
Sofia	Julio	Matt	Erica
Sofia	Erica	Julio	Matt
Sofia	Erica	Matt	Julio
Sofia	Matt	Julio	Erica
Sofia	Matt	Erica	Julio
Julio	Erica	Matt	Sofia
Julio	Erica	Sofia	Matt
Julio	Matt	Sofia	Erica
Julio	Matt	Erica	Sofia
Julio	Sofia	Matt	Erica
Julio	Sofia	Erica	Matt
Erica	Matt	Sofia	Julio
Erica	Matt	Julio	Sofia
Erica	Sofia	Matt	Julio
Erica	Sofia	Julio	Matt
Erica	Julio	Matt	Sofia
Erica	Julio	Sofia	Matt

Assessment Note
Children's work on any of the
problems in this section can be
assessed using the 3-point rubric
on page ix.

Section 4 What Questions Can You Answer?

In this section, children are presented with situations that include numerical data and are asked to generate questions that can be answered from the data. There is a natural integration of language arts and mathematics as students analyze information, formulate and record their questions, and then find the answers to the questions they've created.

It is recommended that the first problem in this section be used as a whole-class activity.

The procedures outlined in the first problem will help children understand how to

a) identify the information that is given in the problem,

b) determine what questions can be answered from the data,

c) find solutions to the questions posed.

Consider having children work the next two problems in the section with a partner or in small groups. This will allow them to brainstorm ideas to generate as many questions as possible. They can select their best questions to record on their worksheets and then work together to find the solutions. The last two problems may then be assigned to some children as independent work.

After children have completed working on a problem, be sure to discuss the questions generated as well as the answers. Such discussion can provide a valuable opportunity for children to hear the variety of questions posed.

Mathematical Skills
....

Problem 1
Money, Addition, Subtraction

Problem 2
Measurement, Addition, Subtraction, Comparing

Problem 3
Geometry, Ordinal Numbers, Counting

Problem 4
Money, Addition, Subtraction, Interpreting Data

Problem 5
Measurement, Interpreting a Map, Addition, Subtraction

Teaching Problem 1 | # Recycle!

Teaching Goal

As children participate in each lesson in this section, they work together to identify the information given in the problem and then make up questions that can be answered with the given information. In this first lesson, children make up questions about a girl who takes empty cans and bottles to the store and is paid 5¢ for each can and 10¢ for each bottle.

Teaching Plan

1. Present the problem to the class.

2. Read the problem aloud as children follow along.

3. Have children work collaboratively in pairs or in small groups to solve the problem. Point out that there are different ways to go about solving a problem, such as modeling it with manipulatives, acting it out, retelling it (in the child's own words), and by drawing a picture.

4. Lead a whole-group discussion of the problem.

Reading the Problem Aloud

Tell children that they are going to read a number story about a girl named Emma who takes empty cans and bottles back to the store to be *recycled*. Although some children will be familiar with the concept of "recycling," others will need to have it explained to them. Point out that once cans and bottles become empty, they are sometimes recycled, or used again, either for holding drinks or for other purposes. Some stores and recycling centers pay people money for each can and bottle brought in for recycling.

▶ Draw children's attention to the rebus art. Point out that the first picture shows two bags—one is full of empty cans, the other is full

(continued on page 46)

Materials (optional)
....

Empty aluminum cans and plastic bottles or counters to represent cans and bottles

Play money—nickels and dimes

Discuss the Meaning of
....

recycle

empty

container

Name
....

Problem 1 **Recycle!**

Emma takes old cans and bottles to the store.

She gets 5¢ for each .

She gets 10¢ for each .

1. Ask a math question about Emma's cans and bottles .

2. Ask a different math question about the cans and bottles .

Reading the Problem Aloud *continued*

of empty bottles. Read the title of the problem aloud. Tell children to follow along as you read the story.

> Emma takes old cans and bottles to the store.
> She gets 5¢ for each can.
> She gets 10¢ for each bottle.

Point out that teachers usually ask math questions for children to answer. Say that today the children will have the chance to be the teacher and ask some math questions for others in the class to answer.

▶ Read item 1 aloud, **"Ask a math question about Emma's cans and bottles."** Tell children that now they will be a teacher and ask math questions. They can do this by telling a math story about the cans and bottles and then turning the story into a question. Give the following example:

Math Story
Emma took 2 cans to the store yesterday and 3 cans today.

Question
If Emma took 2 cans to the store yesterday and 3 cans today, how many cans did she take all together? *or*
How much money did Emma get for bringing 2 cans to the store yesterday and 3 cans today?

Other questions that children might ask include:

Emma took 1 can and 2 bottles to the store. How many *containers* was that?

How much money does the store pay Emma for 1 can and 1 bottle?

How much less money does Emma get for a can than for a bottle?

How can Emma earn 15¢ by recycling?

Children can ask their math questions of their partners or of others in their group. If empty cans and bottles are available, encourage children to use them to act out the answers to the questions. (If containers are not available, then have children use two kinds of counters or classroom objects to represent them, one kind to serve as "cans" and the other to serve as "bottles.")

As you hear the questions children ask, listen for any that either do not require the use of math to answer or that cannot be answered at all. For example, suppose a child asks, "How much money would Emma get for her empty cola cans and bottles at the store?" You would point out that before this question could be answered we would have to know the number of cans and the number of bottles that Emma brought to the store. (After commenting in this way, allow time for the child to revise the question so that it becomes answerable.)

Encourage children to decide how they would like to record their questions in the given space. They may choose to draw pictures and/or to write number sentences.

► Read item 2: **"Ask a different math question about the cans and bottles."** Direct children to use the back of their worksheets for their "different" question.

Suggest that children whose first question was about numbers of cans and bottles now ask a question about an amount of money. Suggest that those children whose first question was about money now ask a question about numbers of cans and bottles.

. . . .

Almost all children will be able to achieve some level of success with this lesson. The sophistication of questions posed depends on the developmental level of each child.

Section 4

Teaching Problem 2 | # Measuring Veggies

Teaching Goal

Tell children that they are going to read a math story about measuring vegetables to find out how long each one is.

In this lesson, children make up questions about a boy who is using connecting cubes to measure the lengths of a carrot, a stalk of celery, and a cucumber.

Reading the Problem Aloud

Read the title of the problem aloud. Ask if anyone knows what "veggies" are. Have children point to the rebus pictures at the top of the page as you identify the pictures as a *carrot,* a *stalk of celery,* and a *cucumber.* Ask, **What do you think the train of connecting cubes below each veggie shows?** Elicit that each "cube train" shows the length of the veggie above it. Have the class follow along as you read the story aloud.

> **Ben's carrot is 4 cubes long.**
> **Ben's celery stalk is 8 cubes long**
> **Ben's cucumber is 6 cubes long.**

Read item 1 aloud. Tell children that here is another chance for them to be a teacher and ask math questions. They can do this by telling a math story about the veggies that they see and then turning the story into a question. Give the following example:

Math Story
The carrot and the cucumber can be lined up end to end.

Question
How long are the carrot and the cucumber together? *or*
How much longer is the cucumber than the carrot?

Be sure to note the correct way to use cube trains to measure—line up one end of the train with one end of the veggie and then count the number of cubes needed to reach the other end of the veggie.

After you read item 2 aloud, explain that children can use the back of their worksheets to ask still more questions about the story.

Materials
....
Connecting cubes

Discuss the Meaning of
....
veggies
cube train
length of a train

After the Lesson
....
Use these questions as part of a whole-group discussion.

What math questions could you answer about two cucumbers and one carrot?

If the carrot were 1 cube longer, what question could you answer about it and the cucumber?

Which is longer, the celery or the length of the carrot plus the length of the cucumber?

 © Wright Group/McGraw-Hill 0-7622-1347-7

Name
....

Problem 2 **Measuring Veggies**

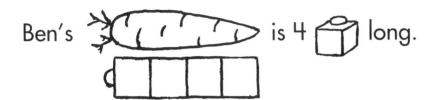

Ben's is 4 long.

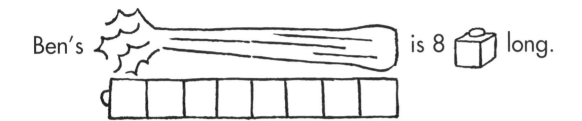

Ben's is 8 long.

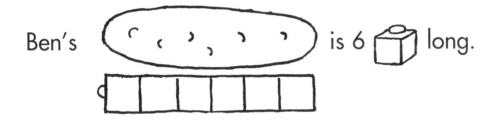

Ben's is 6 long.

1. Ask a math question about Ben's .

2. Ask a different math question about the .

Teaching Problem 3 | # Solid Shapes

Teaching Goal

Tell children that they are going to read a math story about some solid shapes—cubes, cylinders, and pyramids.

In this lesson, children make up questions about pictured cubes, cylinders, and pyramids that appear in various arrangements in three rows.

Reading the Problem Aloud

Read the title of the problem aloud. Display a cube, cylinder, and square-based pyramid (or objects that have these shapes). Allow children to handle the solids. Then encourage children to describe the solids by asking, **What can you tell us about the cube? the cylinder? the pyramid?** Then read, **"Randy put these solids in 3 rows."**

If you have solids available in sufficient numbers so that the three rows can be replicated, ask volunteers to set them up in three rows to match what they see in the picture. Label the rows 1, 2, and 3. Alternatively, have volunteers replicate each row, one at a time.

Read item 1 aloud. Tell children that here is another chance for them to be a teacher and ask math questions. They can do this by telling a math story about the solids and then turning the story into a question. Give the following example:

Math Story
Two solids in row 2 are the same.

Question
Which two solids in row 2 are the same? *or*
Which solid in row 2 is different from the other two?

Children should respond by drawing solids in the space provided or by writing their question or asking you to write it for them as they dictate it to you.

After you read item 2 aloud, explain that children can use the back of their worksheets to ask still more questions about the story.

Materials (optional)
....
Geometric solids: cube, cylinder, square-based pyramid or objects that have these shapes

Discuss the Meaning of
....
solid
cube
cylinder
pyramid

After the Lesson
....
Use these questions as part of a whole-group discussion.

What question could you ask about the solids in row 1? in row 2? in row 3?

What question could you ask about the cubes? about the cylinders? about the pyramids?

What question could you ask about two solids? about three solids? about four solids?

Name

....

Problem 3 **Solid Shapes**

Randy put these solids in 3 rows.

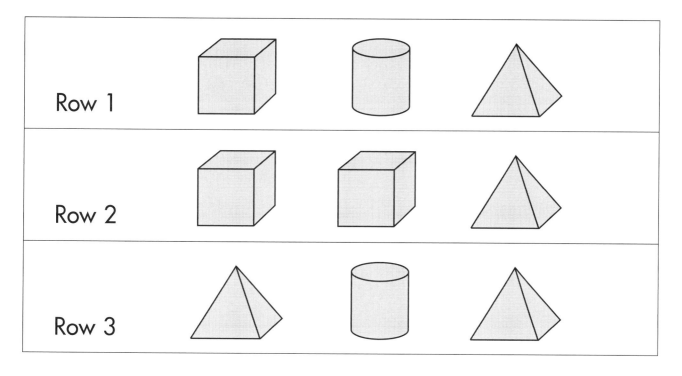

1. Ask a math question about the solids.

2. Ask a different math question about the solids.

Teaching Problem 4 | **Just Desserts**

Teaching Goal

Tell children that they are going to read a math story about four different kinds of desserts.

In this lesson, children make up questions about the cookies, brownies, cake, and fruit tarts that are pictured along with their prices on cafeteria shelves.

Reading the Problem Aloud

Read the title of the problem aloud. Lead a discussion about children's favorite desserts. Point out that there are pictures of some desserts on their worksheets. Elicit that, although we may buy cookies in boxes or bags to bring home, sometimes we buy just one cookie at a time. Ask, **How much does one of the cookies in the picture cost?** Write "10¢" on the board. Have children identify the other desserts pictured and the price of one of each. (You may need to identify the fruit tart as a small pie with fruit on top.)

Read item 1 aloud. Tell children that here is another chance for them to be a teacher and ask math questions. They can do this by telling a math story about the desserts that they see and then turning the story into a question. Give the following example:

Math Story
A brownie costs 15¢ and a tart costs 25¢.

Question
How much more does the tart cost than the brownie? *or*
I bought a brownie for myself and a tart for my sister. How much did I pay?

Children should respond by drawing desserts in the space provided or by writing their question or asking you to write it for them as they dictate it to you. They may also respond by circling the dessert(s) to which their questions refer.

After you read item 2 aloud, explain that children can use the back of their worksheets to ask still more questions about the desserts.

Materials (optional)
....
Play food
Play money

Discuss the Meaning of
....
dessert
fruit tart
cost

After the Lesson
....
Use these questions as part of a whole-group discussion.

What question could you ask about the cookies? the brownies? the pieces of cake? the fruit tarts?

What question could you ask about 15¢ and 20¢? about 10¢ and 25¢?

What question could you ask about all the desserts? (Possible answers: How much would one of each dessert cost? [70¢] If I pay for one of each dessert with a dollar bill, how much change should I get? [30¢])

Problem 4 **Just Desserts**

1. Ask a math question about the sale.

2. Ask a different math question about the sale.

Teaching Problem 5 | # Toy Hunt

Teaching Goal

Tell children that they are going to read a map that shows where one boy's toys can be found.

In this lesson, children interpret a toy-hunt map, which specifies the distances (in numbers of steps) between pairs of toys.

Reading the Problem Aloud

Read the title of the problem aloud. Ask children to name some of their favorite toys. Then ask, **How would you describe where one of your toys is?** Elicit that some descriptions involve measurement.

Arrange three small toys in a triangular configuration on the floor to model the toy-hunt map. Call one volunteer to stand next to one of the toys. Tell that child to walk directly to one of the other toys as the class counts the footsteps aloud. When the child reaches the goal, record the number of steps on the board. Have a second volunteer stand next to a different toy and count and record the footsteps that the child takes to another toy. Repeat the process for the third pair of toys. Summarize children's findings by having children respond to the following question as you ask it *three times*, **How many steps did (child's name) take from the (name of toy) to the (name of toy)?**

Read the story, and then direct children's attention to the Toy Hunt map that Andrew used to find his truck. Elicit that three toys appear on the map—a truck, a magnet, and a flying disk. Point out that the numbers 10, 15, and 20 stand for the number of steps between each pair of toys shown.

Read item 1 aloud. At this point, children should know how to phrase math questions based on given information. They may respond by drawing toys in the space provided or by writing their question or asking you to write it for them as they dictate it to you.

After you read item 2 aloud, explain that children can use the back of their worksheets to ask still more questions about the toy-hunt map.

Materials
....

Toy truck, magnet, and flying disk *or* Three other small toys

Discuss the Meaning of
....

hunt

near

far

After the Lesson
....

Use these questions as part of a whole-group discussion.

What question could you ask about the magnet and the flying disk? the truck and the flying disk? all three toys?

What question could you ask about 15 steps? about 20 steps? (Possible answers: How many steps are there from the truck to the magnet? from the truck to the flying disk?)

Problem 5 **Toy Hunt**

Look at the Toy Hunt map.

See where Andrew found the .

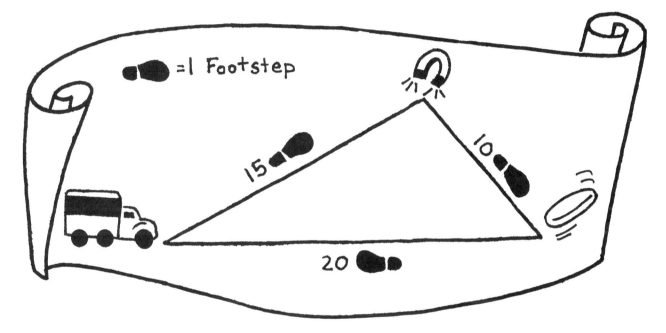

1. Ask a math question about the map.

2. Ask a different math question about the map.

Answer Key

In this section children write questions that can be answered with the information given. This answer key includes typical questions that might be written by children. Many other questions are possible.

Problem 1: Recycle!
Possible questions
How much money will the store pay Emma for 1 can and 1 bottle? (15¢)

How much less does Emma get for a can than for a bottle? (5¢)

How can Emma earn 15¢ by recycling? (By returning 1 can and 1 bottle or 3 cans to the store.)

Problem 2: Measuring Veggies
Possible questions
How much longer is the celery than the carrot? (4 cubes longer)

How many cubes shorter than the cucumber is the carrot? (2 cubes shorter)

If carrots of this size were lined up end to end, how many would be equal in length to a 12-cube train? (3 carrots)

Problem 3: Solid Shapes
Possible questions
How many cubes are in all three rows? (9 cubes)

How many fewer cylinders are there than pyramids? (2 fewer cylinders)

In which row does the same solid come both first *and* last? (row 3)

Problem 4: Just Desserts
Possible questions
How much more does a piece of cake cost than a cookie? (10¢ more)

What can you buy with 25¢? (a fruit tart *or* a cookie and a brownie)

Suppose you have 15¢. Then you find a nickel in your pocket. Which dessert can you buy now? (a slice of cake *or* two cookies)

Problem 5: Toy Hunt
Possible questions
How many steps would it take to get from the magnet to the truck? (15 steps)

How many fewer steps is it from the magnet to the flying disk than from the magnet to the truck? (5 fewer steps)

Suppose you are at the truck and you want to get to the flying disk. How many more steps would you take if you walked past the magnet than if you went straight from the truck to the flying disk? (5 more steps; $15 + 10 = 25$ and 25 is 5 more than 20.)

Assessment Note
Children's work on any of the problems in this section can be assessed using the 3-point rubric on page ix.

 © Wright Group/McGraw-Hill 0-7622-1347-7

Section 5   What's Missing?

IN THIS SECTION, STUDENTS ARE PRESENTED with problems that cannot be solved because an important piece of information has been omitted. Students must identify what is missing, supply appropriate data, and then solve the problem.

It is recommended that the first problem in this section be used as a whole-class activity.

The procedures outlined in the first problem will help students understand how to

a) identify the question that is asked,

b) determine the piece of information that is missing,

c) supply a number or other data that will enable them to solve the problem.

It is suggested that students work the next two problems in the section with a partner or in a small group. Once the majority of students are comfortable with the procedures, they may be able to work the last two problems independently.

Group discussion of problems throughout this section is important, even after students are working independently. Because there is a wide range of data that students can supply to solve each problem, interesting discussions based on the specific data chosen are possible. Each different piece of missing information supplied by a student produces a different solution.

Teaching Problem 1 | # Sticker Sense

Discuss the Meaning of
....
sense
cents

Teaching Goal

As children participate in each lesson in this section, they work together to identify what information is missing from the problem. Then they supply the missing numbers or data they need to solve the problem. In this first lesson, children determine that they cannot answer the question from the given information about the cost of the teddy-bear sticker. They must first supply a price for the kitten sticker. Then they will be able to tell whether or not Maria can buy both a teddy-bear sticker and a kitten sticker with 25¢.

Teaching Plan

1. Present the problem to the class.

2. Read the problem aloud as children follow along.

3. Have children work collaboratively in pairs or in small groups to solve the problem. Point out that there are different ways to go about solving a problem, such as modeling it with manipulatives, acting it out, retelling it (in the child's own words), and by drawing a picture.

4. Lead a whole-group discussion of the problem.

Reading the Problem Aloud

Tell children that they are going to read a number story about a girl named Maria who has 25¢. She wants to use to use the money to buy two stickers. The children must decide if Maria has enough money for the two stickers.

▶ Read the title of the problem aloud. Write the words *sense* and *cents* on the board. Elicit that the two words sound exactly alike. Point to each in turn as you explain that although the words sound the same, they mean different things. Say that the title "Sticker Sense" means that the math story has something to do with

(continued on page 60)

Name

....

Problem 1 **Sticker Sense**

Maria wants to buy a and a .

The costs 15¢.

Maria has 25¢.

Is 25¢ enough for and ?

1. Read the story.

2. Read the question again.

3. Think:

What else do you need to know about the stickers?

4. Pick a price for . _____

5. Now, is 25¢ enough for and ?

Reading the Problem Aloud *continued*

making sense about stickers. The word *cents* refers to money. (Write the cents sign on the board, and tell children to look for it in two places in the story.)

Draw children's attention to the rebus art. Have them identify the teddy-bear sticker and the kitten sticker. Tell them to follow along as you read the following aloud.

Maria wants to buy a teddy-bear sticker and a kitten sticker.

The teddy-bear sticker costs 15¢.

Maria has 25¢.

Is 25¢ enough for the teddy-bear sticker and the kitten sticker?

▶ Read items 1–5 aloud as children follow along. Ask, **What does the problem tell you?** (The price of the teddy-bear sticker and that Maria has 25¢) **Why can't you answer the question?** Be sure children understand that Maria is the girl who is "thinking" the question in item 3. Elicit that, in order to find out if 25¢ is enough money for *both* the teddy-bear sticker and the kitten sticker, children must first answer the question in item 3. (They need to know the cost of the kitten sticker.)

▶ Point out that for item 4, children must decide on a price for the kitten sticker and record that price. Ask, **What could be the price of the kitten sticker? What else could be the price? What other price might make sense?** As children offer various prices, be sure that they understand that there is a range of equally correct prices for the kitten sticker. Some children may say that the kitten sticker should cost the same as the teddy-bear sticker. Others may assign it a price based on its size. Have children give their reason for picking each price.

▶ Finally, have children answer the question in item 5 based on the price they assigned to the kitten sticker for item 4. Ask, **If Maria pays your price for the kitten sticker, will 25¢ be enough for one teddy-bear sticker and one kitten sticker?** (Since the teddy-bear sticker costs 15¢, any price that children assign to the kitten sticker of 10¢ or less should generate a "yes" answer. Any price above 10¢ should generate a "no" answer.)

....

If time allows, have groups of children act out the problem using play money and cutouts of the two kinds of stickers. Have one child in each group be "Maria" (or "Marty"). Give that child a total of 25¢ in play coins. Write "15¢" on the teddy-bear sticker. Then have each of the other children in the group pick a price for the kitten sticker. For each price named, let the group decide whether 25¢ would be enough money to buy both stickers.

Section 5

Teaching Problem 2 | # Nick's Age

Teaching Goal

Tell children that they are going to find the answer to a math question that a boy named Nick asks.

In this lesson, children are challenged to answer a question about how old "Nick" will be in 5 years. They should realize that they must first supply the missing information—Nick's present-day age. They will then add 5 to this number to determine how old Nick will be in 5 years.

Reading the Problem Aloud

Read the title of the problem and the first line of the story aloud. Then say that the boy near the top of the page is Nick and that he is asking this question:

How old will I be 5 years from today?

Call on a few children to be "Nick" (or "Nicole") and to ask the question again and again. Now tell the rest of the class to think about how they could figure out how old each of these children will be 5 years from today.

Read item 1 and item 2 aloud as children follow along. Be sure that they understand that Nick is "thinking" the question in item 2. Ask, **Why can't you tell how old Nick will be in 5 years from today?** (You can't tell because you don't know how old he is today.)

Elicit that in order to find out how old Nick will be in 5 years, children must first respond to item 3. (That is, they need to decide how old Nick is today.) Ask, **How old do you think Nick is today?**

Read the question in item 4 aloud. Ask, **Based on the age you picked for Nick, how old will he be in 5 years?**

> **Discuss the Meaning of**
> ....
> *age*
>
> **After the Lesson**
> ....
> Use these questions as part of a whole-group discussion.
>
> **How old will you (or your brother, sister, or friend) be in 5 years?**
>
> **How old were you (or your brother, sister, or friend) 5 years ago?**

Problem 2 **Nick's Age**

Nick has a question for you.

How old will I be
5 years from today?

Work with a partner.

1. Read the question again.

2. Think:

What else do
you need to know
about me?

3. Pick an age for today.

Nick is _____ years old today.

4. Now, how old will Nick be in 5 years?

He will be _____ years old.

Teaching Problem 3 | # Janet's Purse

Teaching Goal

Tell children that they are going to help figure out how much money a girl has in her purse after some coins fell out of it.

In this lesson, children must supply the missing information—which coins fell out of a purse. They will then find how much money was in the purse at first and subtract the value of the coins that fell out.

Reading the Problem Aloud

Read the title of the problem. Draw attention to the picture of the purse and explain that Janet keeps her money in it.

Now have children follow along as you read the story aloud.

> **Janet had 5 nickels and 5 pennies in her purse.**
> **Then 2 coins fell out!**
> **How much money was in the purse then?**

As children watch, drop 5 nickels and 5 pennies into a purse (or other container). Now slowly tip the purse until two coins fall out. Have children identify the coins. Repeat this a few times so that children understand that each time two different coins may fall out.

Read items 1–3 aloud as children follow along. Be sure that they understand that Janet is "thinking" the question in item 3. Elicit that, in order to find out how much money was left in the purse, children must first answer Janet's question in item 3. (That is, they need to know which two coins fell out.)

After reading item 4, explain that the two circles stand for the two coins that fell out of Janet's purse. Tell children to decide which two coins they are. Say, **If you think two nickels fell out, mark 5¢ on both circles. If you think two pennies fell out, mark 1¢ on both circles. If you think one nickel and one penny fell out, mark 5¢ on one circle and mark 1¢ on the other.**

To answer item 5, children find out how much money was in the purse *before* two coins fell out. Then, they must take away value of the two coins they marked to answer the questions.

Materials (optional)
....

Play money
Purse, or other container for holding money

Discuss the Meaning of
....

money
coins
how much money
subtract
take away

After the Lesson
....

Use these questions as part of a whole-group discussion.

How much are five pennies worth?

How much are five nickels worth?

Would Janet have more money left in her purse if two pennies fell out or if two nickels fell out?

Name ....

Problem 3 **Janet's Purse**

Janet had 5 and 5 in her purse.

Then 2 coins fell out!

How much money was in the purse then?

Work with a partner.

1. Read the story.

2. Read the question again.

3. Think:

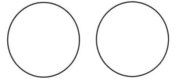

What else do you need to know about the coins that fell out?

4. Pick which 2 coins fell out. ⭘ ⭘

5. Now, how much money was in the purse

after the 2 coins fell out? _____

Teaching Problem 4 | **Cookies and Milk**

Teaching Goal

Tell children that they are going to help find how long it will take a boy to finish eating all the cookies in a box.

In this lesson, children first read about a boy whose mom shows him a full box of cookies. Children are asked to determine how many days it will take until the box is empty. Before they can answer the question, they must first specify how many cookies make up a full box.

Reading the Problem Aloud

Read the title of the problem. Encourage children to talk about the number of cookies that they usually have with their milk. Elicit that two is a reasonable number of cookies to have in a day. Tell children to follow along as you read aloud:

> **Mom shows Mario a box full of cookies.**
> **He may have 2 cookies every day with his milk.**
> **How many days will it take Mario to eat all the cookies?**

Read items 1–3 aloud. Explain that Mario is "thinking" the question in item 3. Elicit that to find out how many days it will take Mario to eat all the cookies, children must first answer his question.

Read item 4, and then encourage children to name a reasonable number of cookies that could fill a box. **Would 3 cookies be enough to fill the box? Would 50 cookies fit into the box?** Elicit reasonable numbers of cookies that could fill the box to answer item 4. To answer item 5, children must figure out how many pairs of (2) cookies Mario can get from that box.

You may wish to create a class chart with headings as follows.

Cookies in Full Box	Eaten Each Day	Cookies Left in Box	Number of Days
?	2	?	?

Note that if an odd number of cookies is in the full box, Mario will have just one cookie to eat on the last day.

Materials (optional)
....

Counters
Small box that holds
about 20 counters
Empty cookie boxes

Discuss the Meaning of
....

full

empty

After the Lesson
....

Use these questions as part of a whole-group discussion.

If there are 10 cookies in the full box, how many days will it take Mario to eat all the cookies? 5 days

If there are 9 cookies in the full box, how many days will it take Mario to eat all the cookies? 5 days

---

Name

Problem 4 **Cookies and Milk**

Mom shows Mario a .

He may have 2 cookies every day with .

How many days will it take Mario to eat all the cookies?

Work with a partner.

1. Read the story.

2. Read the question again.

3. Think:

What else do you need to know about the box of cookies?

4. Pick a number of cookies for the full box.

_____ cookies

5. Now, how many days will it take Mario

to eat all the cookies? _____ days

Teaching Problem 5 | # Zoo Visit

Teaching Goal

Tell children that they are going to help find how many children in one class went on a trip to the zoo.

In this lesson, children read that two teachers took their classes to the zoo. Children are asked to determine how many students are in one of the classes. To answer the question, they must first supply the missing information—how many are in the other class.

Reading the Problem Aloud

Read the title of the problem. Encourage children to recall trips that they already have taken. Point out that sometimes two or more classes go on a trip together.

Draw children's attention to the rebus pictures of the teachers, Ms. Johnson and Mr. Lum. Write "53" on the board. Say that 53 is the number of children in both teachers' classes together. Then read the following aloud.

> **Ms. Johnson and Mr. Lum took their classes to the zoo.**
> **53 children went in all.**
> **How many children were from Ms. Johnson's class?**

Read items 1–3 aloud as children follow along. Be sure that they understand that the teachers are "thinking" the question in item 3. Elicit that in order to find out how many children went to the zoo from Ms. Johnson's class, children must first answer the question.

Then encourage children to name a reasonable number of children for Mr. Lum's class. Ask, **Would 5 children be enough for Mr. Lum's class? How about 60?** To answer item 5, children must think about the number of children that they picked for Mr. Lum's class and then subtract, or take away, that number from 53 to find the answer.

Materials (optional)
....
Counters

Discuss the Meaning of
....
subtract
take away

After the Lesson
....
Consider asking the following for several of the numbers that children pick for #4.

If 53 went to the zoo and (number picked) were from Mr. Lum's class, then how many were from Ms. Johnson's class?

Problem 5 **Zoo Visit**

 and took their classes to the zoo.

53 children went in all.

How many children were from class?

Work with a partner.

1. Read the story.

2. Read the question again.

3. Think:

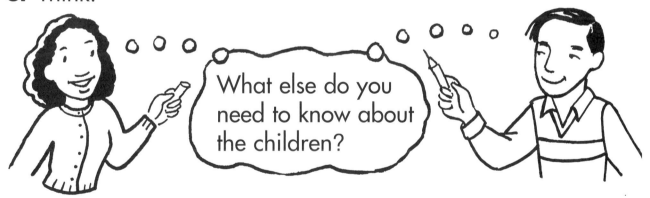

What else do you need to know about the children?

4. Pick a number of children for Mr. Lum's class.

_____ children

5. Now, how many were from Ms. Johnson's class?

_____ children

Answer Key

In this section children read a math problem and determine the kind of missing data that would keep them from solving the problem. Children pick appropriate data with which they can solve the problem (item 4) and then use that data to solve it (item 5). The answers to items 4 and 5 (or items 3 and 4 for Problem 2) will vary depending on the data that children supply.

Problem 1: Sticker Sense
Possible responses:
For items 4 and 5—If the child picks 10¢, then 25¢ would be enough for both stickers.

For items 4 and 5—If the child picks 15¢, then 25¢ would not be enough for both.

Problem 2: Nick's Age
Possible responses:
For items 3 and 4—If the child picks 6, then in 5 years Nick will be 11.

For items 3 and 4—If the child picks 7, then in 5 years Nick will be 12.

Problem 3: Janet's Purse
Possible responses:
For items 4 and 5—If the child picks two nickels, then 20¢ would be left in the purse.

For items 4 and 5—If the child picks two pennies, then 28¢ would be left in the purse.

For items 4 and 5—If the child picks one nickel and one penny, then 24¢ would be left in the purse.

Problem 4: Cookies and Milk
Possible responses:
For items 4 and 5—If the child picks 20 cookies for the full box, then it would take Mario 10 days to eat all the cookies.

For items 4 and 5—If the child picks 15 cookies for the full box, then it would take Mario 8 days— 7 days of eating 2 cookies a day and 1 day of eating 1 cookie.

Problem 5: Zoo Visit
Possible responses:
For items 4 and 5—If the child picks 20 as the number of children that went from Mr. Lum's class, then 33 is the number that went from Ms. Johnson's class.

For items 4 and 5—If the child picks 25 as the number of children from Mr. Lum's class, then Ms. Johnson's class would have sent 28 children.

Assessment Note
Children's work on any of the problems in this section can be assessed using the 3-point rubric on page ix.

Section 6 What's the Question if You Know the Answer?

THE MATHEMATICAL SITUATIONS in Section 6 do not include questions. Children are presented with several possible answers to a given problem situation. They are challenged to supply their own questions for these answers. This section encourages reasoning and the ability to work backward from a specific answer.

It is recommended that the first problem in this section be used as a whole-class activity.

The procedures outlined in the teaching problem will help students learn how to construct a question for a specific answer.

Working in small groups or in pairs is suggested as children learn to compose appropriate questions for the given answers. This will allow them to discuss their thinking with one another. Once children are comfortable with the process, they may be able to work independently.

Whole-group discussion is especially important in this section, even after children are working independently. A question based on specific information can be framed in various ways. Discussing what makes a good question and seeing well-constructed questions modeled will help children become more proficient at writing their own good questions. Children should also talk about how they arrive at a given question. Knowing how to obtain the answer is crucial when constructing the question. It is important for the teacher as well as children to hear the thinking verbalized.

Section 6

Teaching Problem 1 | **Shape Questions**

Teaching Goal

As children participate in each lesson in this section, they generate a variety of questions based on a selection of "answers." In this first lesson, children study 12 figures that represent three different shapes that are shaded in two ways. Then they read answers to yet unstated questions about the figures and decide on a question to pose that would yield each answer.

Teaching Plan

1. Present the problem to the class.

2. Read the problem aloud as children follow along.

3. Have children work collaboratively in pairs or in small groups to solve the problem. Point out that there are different ways to go about solving a problem, such as modeling it with manipulatives, acting it out, retelling it (in the child's own words), and by drawing a picture.

4. Lead a whole-group discussion of the problem.

Reading the Problem Aloud

Tell children that they are going to read a math story about some figures that a girl named Pam sees.

▶ Discuss the group of 12 figures that appear on the worksheet. Elicit that they represent three different kinds of shapes—circles, squares, and triangles—some shaded and others dotted. Elicit that there are 6 circles, 4 squares, and 2 triangles.

Encourage children to describe the similarities and differences among the shapes. Note that someone may (correctly) identify the square as being a "rectangle." If this happens, draw a rectangle on the board and point out that a rectangle has 4 sides and 4 square corners. Then say that a square is a special kind of rectangle

(continued on page 74)

Materials (optional)
....
Attribute Blocks—circles, squares, and triangles, each in two colors

Discuss the Meaning of
....
circle
square
triangle
first, second, third, fourth, fifth

Name
....

Problem 1 **Shape Questions**

Pam sees these shapes.

She asks a question about them.

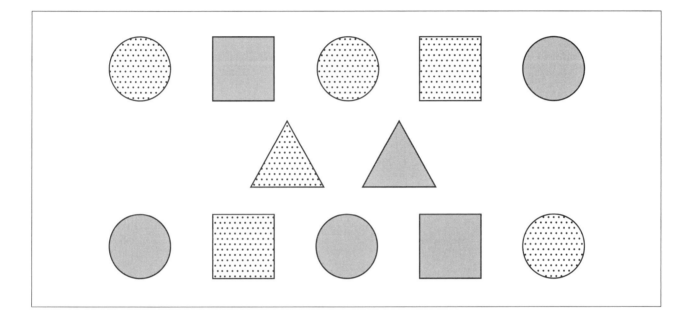

What is Pam's question?

1. If the answer is <u>2</u>, the question could be...

How many △ are there?

2. If the answer is <u>6</u>, the question could be...

3. If the answer is <u>a circle with dots</u>, the question could be...

4. If the answer is <u>12</u>, the question could be...

Reading the Problem Aloud *continued*

because it not only has 4 sides and 4 square corners, but all its sides are exactly the same length.

If Attribute Blocks are available, have children use blocks of two colors to copy the arrangement of the shapes on their worksheets. For example, with a single set of Attribute Blocks, one group of children could copy the pictured figures by using small blue circles, squares, and triangles to stand for the shaded shapes and small yellow circles, squares, and triangles to stand for the dotted shapes. At the same time, another group of children could use two colors of the large circles, squares, and triangles from the set to copy the pictured figures. Suggest that children talk about the shapes with their partners or within their groups. Reinforce children's understanding of ordinal numbers by encouraging them to identify the shapes in the top and bottom rows according to their positions, from first to fifth.

► Read the title of the problem and the first two lines of the story aloud. Explain that the girl in the picture is Pam. Say that she is asking a question…*about a question!* Have children point to Pam's words as you read them aloud.

What is Pam's question?

► Tell children to pretend that you are "Pam" as you read her question. Read item 1, **"If the answer is 2, the question could be…"** Explain that, since 2 of the shapes are triangles, a good question for this answer could be "How many triangles are there?" Ask, **What other question could have the answer "2"?** (How many shaded squares are there? How many dotted squares are there?)

▶ Read items 2–4 aloud. Then, depending on children's abilities, allow them to determine their answer to the questions by working in pairs or in groups. Be sure that it is understood by at least one member of each pair or by at least some of the members of each group that a question must be posed for each given answer. Suggest that children try to think of more than one question for each answer. For some answers, several questions are possible. For others, just one question is possible.

Allow sufficient time for children to compose their questions. Then review children's questions for each of items 1–4. For each, ask, **How did you decide on your question? Can anyone think of another question for that answer?**

▶ As an extension activity, you might ask the more capable children to use the Attribute-Block rectangles and hexagons of two colors and two sizes to create their own arrangement of 12 figures. Groups could give "answers" to questions that they make up and then challenge others to supply appropriate questions for their answers.

Teaching Problem 2 | # Pool Party

Teaching Goal

Tell children that they are going to read a math story about people that a boy named Tony sees at a swimming pool.

In this lesson, children study a picture of 11 people at a swimming pool. They determine the numbers of boys, girls, and adults that are present. Then they read answers about the picture to yet unstated questions and decide on a question to pose that would yield each answer.

Materials (optional)
....
Counters
Plates or bowls

After the Lesson
....
Use these questions
as part of a whole-group
discussion.

**What question could
have the answer 2?**
How many adults/women
are there at the pool?

**How did you decide on
each question?**

**How did you know if
there could be more
than one question for
an answer?**

Reading the Problem Aloud

Read the title of the problem and the first two sentences aloud. Lead a discussion about the people at the swimming pool. (You may wish to have children use counters of three colors to model the three groups of people—boys, girls, and adults/women.) Elicit that there are 5 boys, 4 girls, and 2 women, or adults. Explain that a boy named Tony is also looking at this picture. Say that he is asking a question. Have children point to the question as you read it.

What is Tony's question?

Read item 1 aloud, **"If the answer is 1, the question could be…"** Elicit that since 5 is 1 more than 4, with 5 boys and 4 girls there is 1 more boy than girl in the pool. So, a possible question for the answer 1 is "How many more boys are there than girls?"

Read items 2–4 aloud. Have children compose their question for each answer. Suggest that they try to think of more than one question for each. For some answers, several questions are possible. For others, just one question is possible.

Name

···

Problem 2 **Pool Party**

Tony sees these people.
He asks a question about them.

What is Tony's question?

1. If the answer is 1, the question could be... ○ ○ ○

> How many more boys
> are in the pool than girls?

2. If the answer is 9, the question could be...

3. If the answer is 11, the question could be...

4. If the answer is 7, the question could be...

Teaching Problem 3 | # A Fish Story

Teaching Goal

Tell children that they are going to read a math story about two girls who have used worms to help them catch fish.

In this lesson, children study the pictures of two girls who had been fishing. One girl has used 10 worms to catch 3 fish. The other girl has used 8 worms to catch 2 fish. Children read answers about the story to yet unstated questions and then decide on a question to pose that would yield each answer.

Reading the Problem Aloud

Read the title of the problem and the first two sentences aloud. Lead a discussion about what the two girls, Beth and Dina, are doing. Elicit that they had been fishing. Beth has caught 3 fish and Dina has caught 2. Explain that if a worm is put at the end of a fishing line, any fish that swims by may stop and try to eat the worm. When this happens, the fishing line moves and if the line is pulled out of the water…a fish who has eaten the worm might be caught on the other end! Point out that sometimes fish eat the worms but don't get caught themselves. This is why Dina used 10 worms but caught only 3 fish and why Beth used 8 worms but caught only 2 fish.

Explain that the boy in the picture is Ernie. Say that he is asking a question and that the girls are giving Ernie an answer. Have children point to the question as you read it.

What is Ernie's question?

Read item 1 aloud, **"If the answer is 5 fish, the question could be…"** Elicit that 5 is the total number of fish that the girls caught. So, a possible question for the answer 1 is "How many fish did Beth and Dina both catch?"

Read items 2–4 aloud. Have children compose their question for each answer. Suggest that they try to think of more than one question for each. For some answers, several questions are possible. For others, just one question is possible.

Materials (optional)
....
Counters

Discuss the Meaning of
....
fishing

After the Lesson
....
Use these questions as part of a whole-group discussion.

What question could have the answer 1?
(Possible answer: How many more fish did Beth catch than Dina?)

How did you decide on each question?

How did you know if there could be more than one question for an answer?

Name
....

Problem 3 **A Fish Story**

Ernie sees Beth and Dina fishing.
He asks a question.

I used 10 worms.

I used 8 worms.

Beth

Dina

What is Ernie's question?

1. If the answer is <u>5 fish</u>, the question could be...

How many fish did Beth and Dina both catch?

2. If the answer is <u>2 worms</u>, the question could be …

3. If the answer is <u>Beth</u>, the question could be …

4. If the answer is <u>Dina</u>, the question could be …

Teaching Problem 4 | # Class Votes

Teaching Goal

Tell children that they are going to read a math story about which pet one class would like to have in their room.

In this lesson, children interpret a pictograph that reflects a class's votes for a new class pet. Children read answers about the story to yet unstated questions and then decide how to pose a question that would yield each answer.

Reading the Problem Aloud

Read the title of the problem, along with the first two sentences, aloud. Lead a discussion about what it means to vote. Elicit that the children in one class voted for one of four possible new pets—a turtle, a rabbit, a hamster, or a goldfish.

Draw children's attention to the pictograph on their worksheet. Help them understand that the smiley faces to the right of each pet stand for the votes for that pet. (Be sure to explain that each smiley face stands for one vote.) It may help children to read the graph if they hold a sheet of paper below each row of the graph.

Explain that the teacher in the picture is asking a question. Have children point to the question as you read it.

What is the teacher's question?

Read item 1 aloud, **"If the answer is 1, the question could be…"** Elicit that there is 1 more vote for a rabbit than a hamster. So, the question **"How many more children voted for a rabbit than a hamster?"** has 1 as the answer. (Another question with the same answer is "How many more children voted for a rabbit than a goldfish?")

Read items 2–5 aloud. Have children compose their question for each answer. Suggest that they try to think of more than one question for each. For some answers, several questions are possible. For others, just one question is possible.

Materials (optional)
....
Counters

Discuss the Meaning of
....
vote

After the Lesson
....
Use these questions as part of a whole-group discussion.

What question could have the answer 3? (Possible answer: How many fewer children voted for a turtle than a rabbit?)

How did you decide on each question?

How did you know if there could be more than one question for an answer?

Problem 4 **Class Votes**

The children voted for a new class pet.
The teacher asks a question.

Key: ☺ = 1 child

Turtle	🐢	☺ ☺ ☺ ☺
Rabbit	🐰	☺ ☺ ☺ ☺ ☺ ☺ ☺
Hamster	🐹	☺ ☺ ☺ ☺ ☺ ☺
Goldfish	🐟	☺ ☺ ☺ ☺ ☺ ☺

What is the teacher's question?

1. If the answer is 1, the question could be...

How many more children voted for a rabbit than a hamster?

2. If the answer is 2, the question could be …

3. If the answer is 10, the question could be …

4. If the answer is 13, the question could be …

5. If the answer is goldfish and hamster, the question could be …

Teaching Problem 5 | # Saturday Chores

Teaching Goal

Tell children that they are going to read a math story about a girl who helps around the house by doing chores on Saturdays.

In this lesson, children study the pictures that show Tori engaged in doing five different chores. Each chore is marked with the length of time that it takes to complete it. Children read answers about the story to yet unstated questions and then decide on a question to pose that would yield each answer.

Reading the Problem Aloud

Read the title of the problem. Lead a discussion about what the children in your class typically do on Saturdays. Elicit that Saturday is not a school day. It is not a workday for some people, and so they may spend that day in different ways. Explain that some people do chores, or tasks, on Saturdays that they don't have time to do on other days.

Read the first two sentences of the story aloud. Call on volunteers to describe what Tori is doing in each picture. After each description ask **How many minutes does Tori spend on that chore?** Then say that Tori's dad is asking a question. Have children point to the question as you read it.

What is Dad's question?

Read item 1 aloud, **"If the answer is put toys away, the question could be…"** Have children point to the picture that shows Tori putting a toy away. Elicit that a possible question for this answer is **"Which chore takes Tori 5 minutes less than sweeping?"** (Another question with the same answer is "Which one chore takes 15 minutes to complete?")

Read items 2–4 aloud. Have children compose their question for each answer. Suggest that they try to think of more than one question for each. For some answers, several questions are possible. For others, just one question is possible.

Materials (optional)
....

"Clockworks" clock (or other clock with movable hands)

Discuss the Meaning of
....

Saturday
chore

After the Lesson
....

Use these questions as part of a whole-group discussion.

What question could have the answer 70 minutes, or 1 hour 10 minutes? How much time does Tori spend on all her Saturday chores?

How did you decide on each question?

How did you know if there could be more than one question for an answer?

Name
....

Problem 5 **Saturday Chores**

Tori spends time doing chores on Saturday.
Dad asks a question.

| 10 minutes | 15 minutes | 20 minutes | 5 minutes | 20 minutes |

What is Dad's question?

1. If the answer is <u>put toys away</u>, the question could be...

Which chore takes Tori
5 minutes less than sweeping?

2. If the answer is <u>sweep the floor and help Mom with dinner</u>,

the question could be...

3. If the answer is <u>5 minutes</u>, the question could be...

4. If the answer is <u>25 minutes</u>, the question could be...

Answer Key

Problem 1: Shape Questions

Possible responses:

1. How many more squares are there than triangles?
2. How many circles are there?
3. What is the last shape in the bottom row?
4. How many figures are there in all?

Problem 2: Pool Party

Possible responses:

1. How many more boys are there than girls?
2. How many boys and girls are there in all?
3. How many people are at the pool?
4. How many boys and women are at the pool?

Problem 3: A Fish Story

Possible responses:

1. How many fish did the two girls catch together?
2. How many more worms did Beth use than Dina?
3. Which girl caught more fish?
4. Which girl caught fewer fish?

Problem 4: Class Votes

Possible responses:

1. How many more children voted for a rabbit than for a hamster?
2. How many fewer votes were there for a turtle than for a goldfish?
3. How many votes were there in all for a turtle and a hamster?
4. How many votes were there in all for a rabbit and a hamster?
5. Which two kinds of pets got an equal number of votes?

Problem 5: Saturday Chores

Possible responses:

1. Which chore takes Tori 5 minutes more than making her bed?
2. Which two chores take Tori 40 minutes?
3. How much more time does it take Tori to sweep than to put her toys away?
4. How much time does it take Tori to make her bed and put her toys away?

Assessment Note

Children's work on any of the problems in this section can be assessed using the 3-point rubric on page ix.